31 DAYS of GOD's LOVE-CALL

*My Beloved,
I made you, I know you, and I love you.*
— *God*

31 Days of God's Love-Call:
Pocket Edition
Copyright © 2016, 2023
Stephen Joseph Wolf
All rights reserved.
No part of this book may be copied or reproduced in any form or by any means without the written permission of the publisher, except for the inclusion of brief quotations in a review.

Stephen Joseph Wolf is retired, a former parish priest (22 lents & holy weeks), spiritual director and retreat leader, and former certified public accountant (14 tax seasons), and before that worked as a landscaper, desk clerk, laundry worker, janitor, paper boy, and student.

For more visit **www.idjc.org.**

Printed and distributed by Ingram Books.

ISBN 978-1-937081-46-1

See ***A Jesus Breviary*** for all 8 in 1.
- 31 Days of God's Love-Call
- 31 Days of Jesus Incarnate
- 31 Days of Jesus Miracles
- 31 Days of Jesus Parables
- 31 Days of Jesus Sayings
- 31 Days of Jesus' Paschal Mystery
- 31 Days of the Holy Spirit
- 31 Days on the Christian Life

and ***Rainbow Prayer, Dawn & Dusk Rainbow Prayer,***
and ***Dawn & Dusk Rainbow Prayer for Ordinary Time***

introduction

What do you hear when you read God's word in the Bible? I hear a very long love letter. The Bible as a whole can be read in this simple message from God:

I made you, I know you, and I love you.

This can be a message of great consolation. If I am aware of not living as if God loves me, it can nudge as a challenge, not to be better to earn God's love, but a reminder of my desire to live a fidelity response to God's complete love for me.

It has been an honor to journey with many good folks in the *Spiritual Exercises* of St. Ignatius of Loyola in At-Home Retreats and in spiritual direction. The first part of the exercises is to sit with intention in the reality of God's provision and love. This means letting God say and repeat, *I love you*. These 31 passages rendered here without commentary can help let this message sink into one's being.

Though most of them are psalms and canticles to sing to God, as scripture they are also meant to be read as part of God's revelation; so whether the words are addressed to God, to someone else, or to the reader, we can hear them as God's love letter to us.

The ancient way of listening to God in *lectio divina* can be as simple as choosing a word or phrase or image from the passage, sitting with it perhaps without thinking about it, and breathing to listen.

All God's Blessings,

Steve Wolf

God's Love

for you and for me is complete,
and our God is calling us.

Each person is created
to praise, revere, and serve our Lord God,
and in this vocation
to find salvation in eternal life.

The other things on the face of the earth
are created for us all, to help each person
find and fulfill the *purpose/reason/end/...*
for which he or she is created.

We humans are to use well the other things
to the extent they help us discover and fulfill
our *purpose/reason/end/...*

Sooner or later each of us
will need to rid ourselves of the other things
that get in the way of this personal vocation.

It will come to be our desire
to be indifferent to all created things,
as far as we are allowed free choice
and consistent with faithful commitments
already freely made.

And so, our concern will be to see
all good things in unbiased balance,
and we will not prefer
health to sickness,
riches to poverty,
the world's honor to its dishonor,
or a long life to a short life,
and this balance of indifference
will hold for all other things.

When my one desire comes to be
whatever is more conducive
to the *purpose/reason/end/…*
for which I am created,
may my choices reflect that desire.
If not now, when?

The Principle and Foundation
of St. Ignatius of Loyola, d. 1556
is usually part of the first days of
The Spiritual Exercises (para. 23).

1

God, you are my God;
you I earnestly seek.
My soul, she thirsts for you,
my body, he longs for you,
as in a land with no water,
dry and weary.
So in the sanctuary I saw you,
beheld you in your power and glory.
Your love is better than life itself;
my lips will glorify you.
So I will praise you
in all the ways I am alive;
in your name I will lift up my hands.
As with fatness and richness,
my soul will be satisfied;
with singing lips
my mouth will sing praise.
When I remember you on my bed,
through night watches I think of you,
you who are my help;
then in the shadow of your wings I sing.
My very self stays close to you;
your right hand upholds me.

Psalm 63:1-8

2

God is our refuge and strength,
our help in troubles, ever present.
And so we will not fear,
even if earth were to give way,
even if mountains were to fall
into the heart of the sea,
even if sea waters foam
or mountains quake with a surging.
Streams of a river make glad the city of God,
the holy dwelling place of the Most High.
God is inside her and she will not fall.
God will help her at the break of day.
Nations are in uproar, kingdoms fall;
the earth melts at the voice of God.
Come and see the works of my Lord,
the desolations brought on the earth:
making wars to cease to the ends of the earth,
breaking the bow and shattering the spear
and burning with fire the chariot and shield.
"Be still! And know that I am God.
 I will be exalted among the nations;
 I will be exalted on the earth."
My Lord, the God of Hosts is with us;
the God of Jacob is our fortress.

Psalm 46

3

Yes! All you thirsty,
come to the waters!
And you who have no money,
come! Buy! And eat!
And come with no money
and buy wine and milk at no cost!
Why spend money on what is not bread,
and your earnings on what does not satisfy?
Listen! Listen to me and eat the good,
and your soul will delight in the richness.
Give your ear, and come to me!
Hear, that your soul may live!
I will make with you an everlasting covenant,
the faithful loves of David.
See, a witness to the peoples I made him,
leader and commander of peoples.
Surely you will summon
a nation you do not know,
and nations that do not know you
will hasten to you
because of the Lord your God,
and to the Holy One of Israel
who endowed you with glory.
While the Lord can be found, seek!
And while near, call!

Let the doers of bad forsake their ways,
and the thinker of bad things turn to the Lord
who will have mercy,
and to our God who makes great to pardon.
"For my thoughts are not your thoughts,
 and nor are your ways my ways,"
declares the Lord;
"For as the heavens are higher than the earth,
 so are my ways higher than your ways
 and my thoughts higher than your thoughts.
 As the rain and the snow
 come down from the heavens
 and do not return there
 without first watering the earth
 and making her to bud fertile and flourish,
 yielding seed to the sower
 and bread to the eater,
 so is the word that goes out from my mouth.
 My word will not return to me empty
 but will accomplish my desire
 and will achieve the purpose
 for which I sent it."

Book of the Prophet Isaiah 55:1-13

4

God of my ancestors, Lord of mercy,
who made all things by your word
and through your wisdom framed humanity
to be master of the creatures you have created
and to govern the world in holiness and justice
and judge justly and with an upright heart,
give me Wisdom,
your companion at the throne, and
do not reject me from among your children,
for I am your servant, born of your handmaid,
a feeble human with a short life
and a weak understanding of justice and laws.
Though one be ever so perfect in human eyes,
without your Wisdom that same one
will be of no account…
With you is Wisdom, who knows your works
and was present when you created the world,
who knows what is pleasing in your eyes and
what is right in accord with your ordinances.
Send her forth from the holy heavens
and dispatch her from your majestic throne,
that she may labor beside and with me
and I may learn what pleases you.
For she knows and understands all things
and will guide me to prudence in my actions.

Solomon in the Book of Wisdom 9:1-6,9-11

5

My Lord is my shepherd;
nothing shall I lack.
My Lord lays me down in green pastures
and leads me beside still quiet waters,
restoring my soul
and guiding me in paths of justice
for the Lord's own namesake.
So when I walk in the deep dark valley
I will not fear for you are with me,
your rod and staff a comfort to me.
A table you prepare before me
in the presence even of enmity.
My head you anoint with oil
and my cup is overflowing.
Surely goodness and love will follow me
all the days of my life
and I will dwell in the Lord's own house
for the length of my days.

Psalm 23

6

Lord, you search me and you know me.
You know my sitting and my rising;
you perceive my thoughts from afar.
You discern my going and my lying down,
and you are familiar with all of my ways.
When a word is not yet on my tongue
you see it, Lord; you know them all.
Behind and before you hem me in
and you lay your hand upon me.
Too wonderful for me is this knowledge,
more lofty than what I can attain.
Where can I go that is away from your Spirit?
Where could I flee from your presences?
If I go up to the heavens, you are there;
if I make a bed in the shadows, you I see!
If I rise on the wings of dawn,
if I settle on the far side of the sea,
even there your hand will guide me
and your right hand will hold me...
If I say, "Surely darkness will hide me
and the night will light around me,"
even darkness will not be dark to you
and night will shine as the day;
as the darkness, so the light.

For you created my inmost beings;
you knit me together in my mother's womb.
I praise you because
I am full of fear and wonder;
my self knows well
how wonderful are your works.
My frame was not hidden from you
when I was made in the secret place,
woven together in the depths of earth.
Your eyes saw my body
and in your book were written and ordained
all the days before the first day was.
How precious to me, God, are your thoughts,
how vast are they, the sums of them;
if countable they number more than the sand.
Awake and still, I am with you.
Search me, God, and know my heart!
Test me, and know my anxious thoughts!
See if there is in me an offensive way,
then lead me in the way everlasting!

Psalm 139:1-18,23-24

7

Now says the Lord,
the One who created you, Jacob,
the One who formed you, Israel,
"Fear not, for I have redeemed you,
 I have called you by name; you are mine.
 When you pass through the waters
 I am with you
 and through the rivers
 they will not sweep you away.
 When you walk through fire
 you will not be burned
 and flames will not consume you.
 For I am the Lord your God,
 the Holy One of Israel, your Savior.
 I give lands as your ransom
 and nations in your stead.
 You are precious in my eyes,
 honored glorious,
 and I love you.
 I will send people in return for you
 and nations in exchange for your life.
 Do not be afraid
 for I am with you."

Book of the Prophet Isaiah 43:1-5a

8

The Lord said to Moses, "See me rain down for you bread from heaven, and the people will go out and gather enough in the day for the day. I will test whether they follow my instruction. On the sixth day they will prepare what they bring in, to be twice what they gather day to day." ...Then Moses told Aaron, "Say to the whole community of sons and daughters of Israel, 'Come before the Lord who has heard your grumblings.'" ...They looked toward the desert, and saw the glory of the Lord appearing in the cloud.

The Lord spoke to Moses, "Tell them I have heard the grumblings of the sons and daughters of Israel, and at evening you will eat meat and in the morning you will be filled with bread; then you will know that I am the Lord your God."

In the evening quail came and covered the camp and in the morning there was a layer of dew around the camp; when the dew went away, they saw on the desert floor thin flaking, thin like frost on the ground. When they saw it, they said to each other, "What is this?" (*man hu?*) They did not know. So Moses said to them, "This is the bread that the Lord has given to you for food."

Book of Exodus 16:4-5,9,10b

9

"She did not acknowledge
 that I gave her grain and new wine and oil,
 and lavished on her the silver and gold
 they used for the "god" Baal.
 So I will turn
 and take away my grain in its time
 and my new wine when it is ready;
 I will take back my wool
 and my linen covering her nakedness.
 I will expose her lewdness
 before the eyes of her lovers
 and no one will take her from my hand.
 I will stop all her celebrations
 and the yearly festival of her New Moon
 and Sabbath days,
 even all her appointed feasts.
 I will ruin her vine and her fig tree
 with which she says her lovers paid her,
 and I will make them into thickets
 the wild animals will devour.
 I will punish her for the days
 she burned incense to the Baal "gods"
 and decked herself in ring and jewelry,
 chasing lovers but forgetting me,"
says the Lord.

"See, I will allure her
 and lead her to the desert
 and speak to her heart.
 There I will give back to her the vineyards
 and make for her a door of hope
 and she will respond there
 as in the days of her youth,
 as in the days when she came
 out of the land of Egypt."

"In that day," declares the Lord,
"you will call me 'husband'
 and no longer call me 'master.'"

"I will remove the names
 of the Baals from her mouth
 and their names will be invoked no longer.
 In that day I will make for them
 a covenant with the beasts of the field
 and with birds of the air
 and creatures on the ground,
 and abolish bow and sword and battle
 from the land so all may rest in safety.
 I will espouse you to me to forever
 in righteousness and justice and love,
 in mercy and compassion and fidelity,
 and you will know me as Lord."

Book of the Prophet Hosea 2:10-22

10

Lord, my heart is not proud
and my eyes are not haughty
and I am unconcerned
with the great matters,
with things so wonderful
as to be beyond me.
But indeed I have become still
and quiet in my soul
like a child with a mother
and being weaned.
Like one being weaned
is my soul within me.
Israel, put your hope in the Lord
from now and to forevermore.

Psalm 131

11

Lord, our Lord!
How majestic is your name in all the earth!
Your glory is set above the heavens!
From lips of children and infants
you ordained strength to bring to silence
enmity, opposition and vengeance.
When I consider your heavens,
the works of your fingers,
the moon and stars which you set in place,
what is a human that you would be mindful,
a child of Adam and Eve that you would care?
And you made us little lower than a "god"
crowning us with glory and honor,
making us to rule over works of your hands,
putting everything under our feet,
flocks and herds, all of them,
and also beasts of the field,
birds of the air, and fishes of the sea
swimming through the paths of the seas.
Lord, our Lord!
How majestic is your name in all the earth!

Psalm 8

12

My soul, praise my Lord!
All my inmost being, praise the holy Name!
My soul, praise my Lord,
whose benefits are not to be forgotten:
forgiveness of all your sins,
healing of all your diseases,
redemption of your life from the pit,
crowning you with love and compassion,
satisfying your desire with good,
renewing your youths like the eagle,
working righteousness and justice
for all who are oppressed.
The ways of my Lord
are made known to Moses
and the deeds to peoples of Israel.
Compassionate and gracious is my Lord,
slow to anger and abundant in love,
neither accusing to always
nor harboring anger to forever,
neither treating us in accord with our sins
nor repaying us in accord with our iniquities.
As high as the heavens are above the earth
so great is the love
for ones who fear my Lord.
As far as the east is from the west
so far from us are our transgressions removed.

As a good father
has compassion on his children,
so has my Lord compassion on ones fearing,
knowing our form
and remembering we are dust.
The days of a human are like the grass
flourishing like flowers of the field,
for wind blows over and it is no more
and the place remembers it no more.
But the love for those who fear my Lord
is from everlasting to everlasting.
The righteousness is for children of the children
of those keeping the covenant
and those remembering to obey the precepts.
My Lord established a throne in the heavens
and rules over all the kingdoms.
Praise my Lord, you angels,
you strong and mighty ones doing the bidding,
obeying the voice of the word.
Praise my Lord, you hosts,
you serving and doing the will.
Praise my Lord, all you works,
in all places of the dominion.
My soul, praise my Lord!

Psalm 103

13

Psalm 104

Soul of me, praise the Lord!
God, my Lord, you are beyond measure.
Splendor and majesty clothe you,
wrapped in light as a garment,
stretching out over the heavens like the tent,
laying beams on the waters
of the upper chambers.
You make a chariot of the clouds,
riding on wings of wind,
making messengers of the winds
and servants of flaming fire.
You have set foundations on earth,
unmovable for ever and ever.
Deep is your garment, covering the earth;
above the mountains the waters stood.
At your rebuke, they then fled;
at the sound of your thunder
they took flight.
They flowed over mountains
and went down into valleys
to the places you assigned for them.
You set a boundary
they are not to cross;
never again are they to cover the earth.

You make springs of water
pour into ravines;
between the mountains they flow.
They give water
to all beasts of the field;
they quench the thirst of donkeys.
Birds of the air
nest in branches beside them;
they give you their song.
You water mountains
from your upper chambers;
by the fruit of your works
the earth is satisfied.
You make grass grow for the cattle
and plants for human beings to cultivate
to bring forth food from the earth,
wine to make glad the human heart,
oil to make faces shine,
and bread to sustain the human heart.
They are all the Lord's well watered trees,
cedars of Lebanon planted
where birds make their nests,
and the pine tree
where the stork makes a home,
mountains, the high ones, for wild goats,
and crags, a refuge for rock-badgers.

Psalm 104, continued

You mark off seasons by the moon,
and know the going down of the sun.
You bring darkness
and all beasts of the forest
prowl in the night.
The lions roar for prey
seeking their food from God.
The sun rises, they steal away,
and into their dens they lie down.
Human beings go out to do their work
and labor until the evening.
How many are your works, Lord!
All of them in wisdom you made.
The earth is full of your creatures.
There is the sea, vast and spacious;
living creatures countless there,
small ones and large ones.
There ships go about
and leviathan which you formed for frolic.
All of them look to you
to give them food at their time.
You give to them and they gather,
you open your hands
and they are goodly satisfied.

You hide your face and they are terrified,
you take away their breath and they die
and to their dust they return.
You breathe your Spirit,
and they are created,
and you renew the faces of earth.
May the glory of the Lord endure to forever.
May the Lord rejoice in the works:
looking at the earth, she trembles,
touching the mountains, they smoke.
I will sing to the Lord during my life
and sing praise to my God while I still am.
May my meditation be found pleasing.
I rejoice in the Lord.
May sin vanish from the earth
and the wicked be so no more.
Praise, my soul, Lord!
Hallelujah!

Psalm 104

14

The heavens declare the glory of God,
and the sky proclaims
the work of God's hands.
Day after day, speech pouring forth,
and knowledge on display night after night.
There is no speech, there is no language,
and no sound is heard.
Into all the earth their line goes out
and their words to the ends of the world.
There God has pitched a tent for the sun,
and like a bridegroom coming forth,
and like a champion running the course,
rejoices.
At the end of the heavens is the rising,
to their furthest ends is the circuit,
and nothing is hidden from its heat.
The law of the Lord is perfect,
reviving the soul;
statutes of the Lord are trustworthy,
making wise of the simple;
precepts of the Lord are right ones,
giving joy of heart;
the command of the Lord is radiant,
giving light to eyes;
the fear of the Lord is pure,
enduring to forever;

the ordinances of the Lord are sure
and altogether just;
more precious than gold,
much more than pure gold,
more sweet than honey,
the honey of honeycombs.
Your servant is being warned by them;
to keep them is a great reward.
Who can discern errors?
From those hidden from me, forgive me!
And keep your servant from willful sins!
May they not rule over me;
then will I be blameless
and innocent of great transgression.
May the words of my mouth be as pleasing
and the meditation of my heart be as pleasing
before you, my Lord,
my Rock and my Redeemer.

Psalm 19

15

Elijah went a day's journey into the desert, sat at a broom tree, and prayed, "Enough, Lord; take my life; I am no better than my ancestors."

He lay and fell asleep under the one broom tree. A messenger touched him and said, "Get up. Eat." He looked up and saw by his head a cake baked on coals and a jar of water. He ate and drank and lay down again.

The angel of the Lord returned and touched him again and said, "Get up. Eat, or the journey is too much for you." He got up and ate and drank and walked in strength of the food for forty days and forty nights to the mountain of God, Horeb. He entered the cave there and spent the night...

The Lord said, "Go and stand on the mountain in the presences of the Lord and see the Lord pass by.

A great and powerful wind tore at the mountain shattering rocks, but the Lord was not in the wind. After the wind, an earthquake, but the Lord was not in the earthquake. After the earthquake, fire, but the Lord was not in the fire. After the fire, a voice in gentle whisper. When Elijah heard it, he covered his faces with his cloak and going out stood at the mouth of the cave.

Elijah in 1 Kings 19:4-9a,11-13

16

The Lord declares,
"I know the plans I plan for you,
 plans for welfare and not for harm
 to give you a future and hope.
 Then you will call upon me
 and you will come
 and you will pray to me
 and I will listen to you
 and you will seek
 and you will find me
 when you seek me with all your heart,
 and I will be found by you
 and I will bring you back from your captivity
 and I will gather you from all the nations
 and from all the places where I sent you,
 and I will bring you back
 to the place from where you were exiled,"
declares the Lord.

Book of the Prophet Jeremiah 29:11-14

17

The Lord says to Jerusalem…"On the day you were born your cord was not cut, nor your body washed with water, anointed, rubbed with salt, or wrapped in swaddling clothes. Not seen by any with pity or compassion, you were thrown into the open field, rejected on the day of your birth. Then I passed by and saw you kicking in your blood and said to you laying there, "Live!" I made you to grow like a plant in the field and you grew and matured to a jewel of jewels. Your breasts formed and your hair covered your nakedness.

Then I passed by again and saw that you were at the time of love, so I spread the corner of my garment over you to cover your nakedness and gave an oath to you and entered into a covenant with you, and you became mine. I bathed you with the waters, washed the blood off you, anointed you with oil, clothed you in embroidery, put on your feet leather sandals, dressed you in fine linen, covered you with expensive clothing, and adorned you with jewelry, bracelets, necklace and ring, earrings, and a beautiful crown. You ate of fine flour, honey and olive oil, and you became very beautiful, indeed a queen."

Book of the Prophet Ezekiel 16:4-13

18

The word of the Lord came to Jeremiah,
saying,
"Get up and go down
  to the house of the potter
  and there I will give you my message."
I went down to the potter's house
and saw him working at the wheel.
When the pot he was shaping from clay
came apart in his hand,
the potter formed the pot again,
shaping it to be
pleasing in the potter's own eyes.
Then the word of the Lord came to me,
"Can I not do with you, house of Israel,
  as this potter has done?"
says the Lord.
"See:
  like clay in the hand of the potter,
  so are you in my hand,
  house of Israel."

Book of the Prophet Jeremiah 18:1-6

19

This is the story of the heavens and the earth when created. The Lord God made earth and heavens □ no shrub nor plant having yet appeared on any field of the earth, nor rain been sent by the Lord God, nor any human to work the ground, but a stream welled up from the earth and watered the whole surface of the ground.

And the Lord God formed the human from dust of the ground and breathed into his nostrils the breath of life and the human became a living being. The Lord God planted a garden in Eden in the east and put there the formed human. The Lord God made grow from the ground every tree pleasant to sight and good for food, and the tree of life in the middle of the garden and the tree of knowledge of good and evil. A river flowed from Eden to water the garden, dividing into four branches…(Pishon, Gihon, Tigris and Euphrates).

The Lord God took and put the human in the garden of Eden to work and care for it, and the Lord God commanded, "You are free to eat from any tree of the garden, but you must not eat from the tree of knowledge of good and evil, for in the day you eat from it you will die."

Book of Genesis 2:4-17

20

God said, "Let the earth bring forth living creatures of every kind, tame and crawling and wild animal of every kind," and it was. God made every kind of wild and tame animal and every kind of mover over the ground. God saw it good.

Then God said, "Let us make the human in our image, in our likeness. Let them rule over the fish of the sea, the birds of the air, the animals tame and wild, and movers moving on the ground." So God created the human in God's image, created in the image of God, male and female God created them.

God blessed them and God said to them, "Be fertile and multiply; fill the earth; subdue her. Rule over the fish of the sea, the birds of the air, and every living thing moving over the ground." God said, "See, I give you every seed-bearing plant that seeds the whole face of the earth and every tree with fruit and seed seeding for food for you, every beast of the earth, bird of the air, thing moving on the ground with life-breath in it, and green plant for food," and it was. God saw all that God made and found it very good.

Evening and morning came, the sixth day.

Book of Genesis 1:24-31

21

Be not afraid, for indeed you will suffer no shame. Fear no disgrace for you will have no humiliation. You will not remember the shame of your youth and forget the reproach of your widowhood. For your One Maker is your husband, named the God of Might, and your Redeemer, the Holy One of Israel, called God of all the earth.

As if a deserted wife who is distressed in spirit, the Lord God will call you back, as a wife of youth then rejected, says your God. For a brief moment I abandoned you but with deep compassion I will bring you back. In a surge of anger, for a moment, I hid my faces from you, but my compassion will rest on you with love that endures, says the Lord God, your Redeemer.

As after the waters of Noah I swore that never would the waters of Noah again cover the earth, so have I sworn to not be angry with you or to rebuke you again.

Though the mountains be shaken and the hills fall, my covenant of peace will never fail and my love for you will not be shaken, says the Lord, who has compassion on you.

Book of the Prophet Isaiah 54:4-10

22

See! I set before you today life and prosperity and death and adversity. My command is to love the Lord your God, in whose ways you are to walk and whose commands and decrees and laws you are to keep. Then you will live and increase, and the Lord your God will bless you in the land you enter to possess.

But if your heart turns away, and you do not obey, and you are led astray, and you bow down to other "gods" and you serve them, I declare to you today that you will perish and you will not have long days in the land you are crossing the Jordan to enter and possess.

I call today as witness against you the heavens and the earth, that I have set before you life and death, blessing and curse. Choose now life, that you and your descendents may live to love the Lord your God, to listen and hold fast to this voice. For the length of the days of your life, dwell in the land the Lord swore to give your ancestors, to Abraham, Isaac, and Jacob.

Moses in the Book of Deuteronomy 30:15-20

23

For the sake of Zion, I will not keep silent;
for the sake of Jerusalem
I will not remain quiet,
till righteousness comes out like the dawn
and salvation blazes like a torch.
The nations will see your righteousness
and all the kings your glory
and you will be called by a new name
that the mouth of the Lord will bestow.
You will be a crown of splendor
in the hand of the Lord
and a royal diadem in the hand of your God.
No longer will you be called
One Being Deserted,
nor will your name be called Desolation,
but you will be called
"my delight is in her"
and your land "espoused."
The Lord will delight in you
and your land will be married.
As a young man marries a maiden,
your Builder will marry you;
and as a bridegroom rejoices over a bride,
so will your God rejoice over you.

Book of the Prophet Isaiah 62:1-5

24

For everything, there is a time, and
a season for every activity under the heavens:
  a time to be born and a time to die,
  a time to plant and a time to uproot,
  a time to kill and a time to heal,
  a time to tear down and a time to build,
  a time to weep and a time to laugh,
  a time to mourn and a time to dance,
  a time to scatter stones and a time to gather,
  a time to embrace and a time to refrain,
  a time to seek and a time to lose,
  a time to keep and a time to throw away,
  a time to tear and a time to mend,
  a time to be silent and a time to speak,
  a time to love and a time to hate,
  a time of war and a time of peace.

    What is the gain from the toil of work? See the burden of busy-ness laid on sons and daughters of humanity by God, who created every thing with beauty in its time, and set eternity in their hearts; yet human beings cannot fathom the work done by God from beginning to end... Nothing to add to it and nothing to take from it, God does it, and humans give reverence.

Qoheleth in the Book of Ecclesiastes 3:1-11,14b

25

My soul finds rest in God alone,
from whom is my salvation,
alone my salvation and my rock,
my fortress never to be shaken greatly.
Until when will you assault a human being,
will you throw down, all of you,
like a leaning wall or a tottering fence?
They fully intend
to topple from the lofty place;
they delight in lies and bless with their mouth
and curse in their heart.
My soul finds rest in God alone,
from whom is my hope,
alone my salvation and my rock,
my fortress not to be shaken.
From God is my salvation and my honor;
my mighty rock and refuge.
Trust in God at all times, people;
pour out your heart to God our refuge.
Sons & daughters of humanity are but a breath;
the so-called great ones are an illusion.
On balanced scales they both rise;
together they are only a breath…
One thing God has spoken, two I have heard:
that to God is strength; to you, Lord, is mercy.

Psalm 62:2-10,12,13a

26

Lord God, it is in your power always
to show great strength.
Who can resist the might of your arm?
The whole cosmos before you
is like one grain that tips the scales,
or a drop of morning dew
falling on the ground.
You show mercy to all,
because you can do all things,
and you overlook sins
that humans may repent.
You love all things that are,
and loathe nothing you have made,
for you would not have fashioned
anything that you hated.
How could anything remain
without your willing it?
Or how would anything be preserved
had it not been called forth by you?
But you spare all things,
for they are yours,
Lord Ruler who love the living;
for your eternal spirit is in all things.

Solomon in the Book of the Wisdom 11:21-12:1

27

One who dwells in the shelter of my God,
in the shadow of Shaddai, will find rest.
I will say of my Lord, my refuge, my fortress:
My trust is in my God, who will save you
from fowler snare, from deadly pestilence.
With the feather of the Lord
you will be covered, and under those wings
you will find refuge, shield and rampart,
the faithfulness of the Lord.
You will have no fear of terror at night
nor of arrows flying by day,
of pestilence stalking in the darkness,
nor of plague that destroys at midday.
A thousand may fall at your side,
and ten thousand at your right hand;
near to you they will not come.
Observe with your eyes, simply watch;
punishment of the wicked you will see.
Make the Lord, who is my refuge,
make my God your dwelling.
Harm will not befall you,
nor will disaster come near your tent.
God's own Angels, the Lord will command
to guard you in all of your ways.
In their hands they will lift you up;
your foot will not strike against the stone…

Because you love me, I will rescue you,
I will protect all who acknowledge my Name.
You will call upon me and I will answer.
I am with you in trouble, deliverance & honor.
In length of days I will satisfy you,
and show you my salvation.

Psalm 91:1-12,14-16

28

I will take you out of the nations
and I will gather you from all the countries,
and I will bring you back into your land.
I will sprinkle on you clean waters,
and you will be clean from all your impurities,
and from all your idols I will cleanse you.
I will give you a new heart
and I will put inside you a new spirit,
and I will take the stone-heart from your flesh
and I will give you a flesh-heart,
and I will put inside you my Spirit
and I will move you to follow my decrees
and my laws you will be careful to keep,
and you will live in
    the land I gave your ancestors,
and you will be my people
and I will be your God.

Book of the Prophet Ezekiel 36:24-28

29

The hand of the Lord was on me, and brought me out by the Spirit of the Lord and set me in the middle of the valley full of bones, and led me among them back and forth, to see many great ones on the floors of the valley and to see the very dry ones, and asking me, "Son of humanity, can these bones live?"

And I said, "Sovereign Lord, you, you know." And then to me, "Prophesy to these bones and say to them, the dry bones, 'Hear the word of the Lord! This the Sovereign Lord says to these bones:

See! I am making breath enter into you and you will come to life, and I will attach to you tendons, and I will make flesh come upon you, and I will cover skin on you, and I will put breath in you, and you will come to life; and then you will know that I am the Lord.'"

So I prophesied as I was commanded, and as I prophesied a noise came with a sight: rattling bones coming together bone to bone. And I saw a sight, tendons on them and flesh appeared, and skin covered them over, but there was no breath in them.

Then saying to me, "Prophesy to the breath! Prophesy, son of humanity, and say to the breath, 'This says Sovereign Adonai:

Come from the four winds, breath, and breathe into these slain that they may live!'"

So I prophesied as I was commanded and the breath entered into them, and they came to life, and they stood up on their feet, a very very vast army.

And then to me, "Son of humanity, these bones are the whole house of Israel. See how they say, 'Our bones are dried up and our hope is gone and we are cut off from ourselves.' Prophesy, therefore, and say to them, 'This says the Sovereign Lord:

See! Opening your graves, I will bring you, my people, up from your graves and I will bring you back to the land of Israel. Then you will know that I am the Lord, when I open your graves and bring you to me, my people, and I will put my Spirit in you and you will live, and I will settle you in your land. Then you will know that the Lord has spoken and I have done it, declares the Lord.'"

Book of the Prophet Ezekiel 37:1-14

30

Comfort, comfort my people, says your God.
Speak to the heart of Jerusalem and proclaim
her servitude is complete, her guilt has been paid,
and she has received from the hand of the Lord
double for all her sins. A voice of one calls:
Make straight in the desert the way of the Lord,
prepare in the wilderness a highway for our God.
Every valley shall be raised up
and every mountain and hill shall be made low,
the rough land level,
and the rugged ground plain.
The glory of the Lord will be revealed
and all of humanity will see together,
for the mouth of the Lord has spoken.
A voice says, cry out. And I say, what shall I cry?
Humanity is as grass, all their glory like a flower;
the grass withers and the flower falls;
as the Lord blows breath on grass, so on humans.
The grass withers and the flowers fall
but the word of our God stands to forever.
Go upon a high mountain, and bring good news:
Here is your God!
See, the Sovereign Lord comes.
Like a shepherd feeding his flock, the Lord
gathers the lambs in his arms and carries them
in his heart and leads gently those with young.

Book of the Prophet Isaiah 40:1-11

31

Out of the depths, my Lord, I cry to you.
Lord, hear my voice.
Let your ears be attentive
to my cries for mercy.
If you, my Lord, kept a record of sins,
Lord, who could stand?
But with you is the forgiveness,
and so you are revered in awe.
I wait, my soul waits for my Lord,
in whose word I put my hope.
My soul waits for the Lord
more than watchers for the morning,
even watchers for the morning.
Put your hope, Israel, in the Lord!
For unfailing mercy-love is from the Lord,
in whom is full redemption,
who will redeem Israel from every sin.

Psalm 130

www.ingramcontent.com/pod-product-compliance
Lightning Source LLC
Chambersburg PA
CBHW021200080526
44588CB00008B/428